Emphatically Emerson

EMPHATICALLY
EMERSON

Gems from the Journals of
Ralph Waldo Emerson

selected & arranged by
Frank Crocitto

with an introduction by
Richard Geldard, PhD

CANDLEPOWER
NEW PALTZ, NY

Emphatically Emerson
Frank Crocitto, ed.

With an introduction by Richard Geldard, PhD.

Designed by David Perry & Kirsten Carle.

©2003 Candlepower

Cover image from *Remembrances of Emerson*, John Albee,
Robert G. Cooke, 1901, NY.

Published by Candlepower
P.O. Box 787
New Paltz, NY 12561

www.candlepower.org

ISBN 1-932037-04-7

*To those whose thirst
is only quenched
by Truth.*

Ralph Waldo Emerson
1803 - 1882

If Washington, Jefferson, Hamilton and Franklin are our Founding Fathers, Ralph Waldo Emerson is our Founding Thinker. Born in 1803 in Boston, Emerson became in his lifetime America's seer and prophet. His collected works, including poems, essays, and extensive journals not only inspired such notable figures as Henry David Thoreau, William James, Walt Whitman, Herman Melville and numerous nineteenth and twentieth century poets, painters and musicians, but also a wide readership of ordinary Americans who found in Emerson a teacher of profound depth and idealism. Without doubt he is our most oft quoted writer.

Emerson was the conscience of his nation and a man of great moral courage. He spoke out against the government's illegal and brutal treatment of the Cherokee Nation, against the transparent aggression of the Mexican War, and, most importantly, against the firmly entrenched institution of slavery. Once he was moved to action from the seclusion of his study in Concord, Massachusetts, he galvanized the abolition movement in the North and moved the country closer to a resolution. For years, he and his friend Henry Thoreau helped ferry escaped slaves through Concord on their way to Canada. In 1850, when the Fugitive Slave Law made such help illegal in Massachusetts, Emerson revolted and exposed the hypocrisy of men like Daniel Webster who sold their consciences for the sake of a temporary compromise with the South.

For most of his life, however, Emerson's work was based on what he called "the infinitude of the private man." In his infamous Divinity School Address, for example, he spoke out against the mindless preaching then typical in New England churches and led a spiritual revolution which is still going on. The great literary critic Harold Bloom calls Emerson the father of American religion. He was that and more.

He taught us to listen to our own inner conscience, not as the selfish desire to 'do our own thing', but as the sober intuition of the heart to rise above circumstances and find the noble path. What he called self-reliance was a dependence on a God who spoke in the silence of individual reflection and not in the mouths of loud self-promoters. He said, "There is nothing sacred at last but the integrity of your own mind."

For all the fame he enjoyed in his lifetime, Emerson was a humble man, a good father and husband and friend, who spent his rich life in the service of individual human self-recovery. Today, when it is harder and harder to find leaders and heroes to admire, Emerson stands as someone who represents the very best of the American spirit.

Why Emerson? Why now? In 2003, on May 25, we will celebrate the bicentennial of the birth of America's greatest literary and spiritual figure. At Emerson's centennial in 1903, the Harvard philosopher William James observed that reading Emerson's works made him feel his greatness as never before, and now, nearly a hundred years later, Emerson is speaking to us again and we need his greatness now even more.

This thoughtful collection from Emerson's journals, so private and yet at the same time so universal, will serve to introduce our Founding Thinker to a new generation of readers. Crocitto has lovingly molded what were merely Emerson's notes to himself into neat morsels of thought, each to be tasted and enjoyed at leisure. They should be enjoyed slowly, rolled on the tongue, chewed thoroughly and absorbed for intellectual and spiritual nourishment. Enjoy.

—Richard Geldard, PhD
Author of *The Spiritual Teachings of Ralph Waldo Emerson*
God In Concord, Emerson's Awakening to the Infinite

There is a strange face
in the Freshman class
whom I should like
to know very much.

He has a great deal of character
in his features and should be
a fast friend
or bitter enemy.

I find myself often
idle, vagrant, stupid and hollow.
This is somewhat appalling and,
if I do not discipline myself
with diligent care,
I shall suffer severely from remorse
and the sense of inferiority
hereafter.

All around me are industrious
and will be great,
I am indolent
and shall be insignificant.

Avert it, heaven!
Avert it, virtue!
I need excitement.

I claim and clasp a moment's respite
from this irksome school
to saunter in the fields
of my own wayward thought.
The afternoon was gloomy
and preparing to snow
dull, ugly weather.
But when I came out
from the hot, steaming, stoved,
stinking, dirty, A-B spelling-school-room,
I almost soared
and mounted the atmosphere
at breathing the free magnificent air,
the noble breath of life.

It was a delightful exhilaration...

I am sick—
if I should die
what would become of me?

We forget ourselves
and our destinies
in health,
and the chief use of temporary sickness
is to remind us of these concerns.

I must improve my time better.
I must prepare myself
for the great profession
I have purposed to undertake.

In twelve days
I shall be
nineteen years old,

which I count
a miserable thing.

Has any other educated person
lived so many years
and lost
so many days?

May 1822, age 18

Why
has my motley diary
no jokes?

Because it is a soliloquy

and every man
is grave
alone.

When a whole nation
is roaring
Patriotism
at the top of its voice,
I am fain to explore
the cleanness
of its hands
and purity
of its heart.

It is my own humor
to despise pedigree.
I was educated to prize it.

The kind Aunt whose cares instructed my youth
(and whom may God reward),
told me oft the virtues of her and mine ancestors.

But the dead sleep
in their moonless night;
my business
is with the living.

All things are double
one against another,
said Solomon.

The whole
of what we know
is a system of compensations.

Every defect
in one manner
is made up in another.

Every suffering
is rewarded;
every sacrifice
is made up;
every debt
is paid.

1826, age 22

I deliberately shut up my books
in a cloudy July noon,
put on my old clothes
and old hat
and slink away to the whortleberry bushes
and slip
with the greatest satisfaction
into a little cowpath
where I am sure I can defy
observation.

This point gained,
I solace myself for hours
with picking blueberries
and other trash of the woods,
far from fame,
behind the birch-trees.

July 1828, age 25

When a man has got to a certain point
in his career of truth
he becomes conscious forevermore that
he must take himself
for better,
for worse,
as his portion,
that what he can get out of his plot of ground
by the sweat of his brow
is his meat,
and though the wide universe is full of good,
not a particle can he add to himself
but through his toil bestowed
on this spot.
It looks to him indeed
a little spot,
a poor barren possession,
filled with thorns,
and a lurking place
for adders and apes
and wolves.
But cultivation will work wonders.
It will enlarge to his eye
as it is explored.
That little nook will swell
to a world
of light
and power
and love.

November 1830, age 27

Trust
to that prompting
within you.
No man
ever got above it.
Men have transgressed
and hated
and blasphemed it,
but no man ever sinned
but he felt it
towering
above him
and threatening him
with ruin.

April 1831, age 27

Heraclitus grown old
complained
that all
resolved itself
into
identity.
That thought
was first his philosophy,
and then his melancholy—
the life he lived
and the death he died.

The things taught
in colleges and schools
are not an education,
but the means
of education.

I do not fear death.
I believe those who fear it
have borrowed the terrors
through which they see it
from vulgar opinion,
and not from their own minds.

My own mind is the direct revelation
which I have from God
and far least liable to mistake
in telling his will of any revelation.
Following my own thoughts,
especially as sometimes
they have moved me in the country...
I should lie down
in the lap of earth
as trustingly
as ever on my bed.

December 1831, age 28

What are your sources
of satisfaction?

If they are meats and drinks,
dress, gossip, revenge,
hope of wealth,
they must perish with the body.

If they are contemplation,
kind affections,
admiration of what is admirable,
self-command,
self-improvement,
then they survive death
and will make you
as happy then
as now.

December 1831, age 28

Books are apt to turn reason out of doors.

You find men talking everywhere
from their memories,
instead of
from their understanding.

If I stole this thought
from Montaigne,
as is very likely,
I don't care.

I should have said the same myself.

Don't trust children with edge tools.

Don't trust man,
great God,
with more power than he has,
until he has learned
to use that little
better.

What a hell should we make of the world
if we could do what we would!
Put a button on the foil
till the young fencers
have learned
not to put each other's eyes out.

Take nothing for granted.

This year I have spent say
$20
in wine and liquors
which are drunk up,
and the drinkers
are the worse.

It would have bought a beautiful print
that would have pleased for a century;
or have paid
a debt.

I have sometimes thought that,
in order to be a good minister,
it was necessary
to leave the ministry.

The profession is antiquated.

In an altered age,
we worship
in the dead forms
of our forefathers.

Were not a Socratic paganism
better than an effete,
superannuated
Christianity?

June 1832, age 29

My aunt had an eye
that went through and through you
like a needle.

"She was endowed,"
she said,
"with the fatal gift
of penetration."

She disgusted everybody
because
she knew them too well.

This strong-winged sea-gull
and striped sheer-water
that you have watched
as they skimmed the waves
under our vault,
they are works of art
better worth your enthusiasm,
masterpieces
of Eternal power...
So sang in my ear
the silver-grey mists,
and the winds and the sea said
Amen.

What
under the sun
canst thou do then,
pale face?

Truly
not much,
but
I can hope.

If the sea
teaches
any lesson,
it thunders this through the throat
of all its winds,
'That
there is
no knowledge
that
is not
valuable.'

How beautiful
to have the church
always open,
so that every tired
wayfaring man
may come in
and be soothed
by all that art can suggest
of a better world
when he is weary
with this.

I am my own comedy and tragedy.

I collect nothing
that can be touched
or tasted
or smelled,
neither cameo, painting, nor medallion;
nothing
in my trunk
but old clothes.

**God
defend me
from ever looking at a man
as an animal.**

All
the mistakes I make
arise
from forsaking my own station
and trying to see
the object
from another person's
point of view.

We are always
getting ready to live,
but never living.

We have many years
of technical education;
then
many years of earning a livelihood,
and we get sick,
and take journeys for our health,
and compass land and sea
for improvement by travelling,
but the work of
self-improvement
—always under our nose—
nearer than the nearest,
is seldom engaged in.

A few, few hours in the longest life.

April 1834, age 30

I remember
when I was a boy
going upon the beach
and being charmed
with the colors and forms
of the shells.

I picked up many
and put them in my pocket.

When I got home
I could find nothing that I gathered—
nothing
but some dry, ugly mussel
and snail shells.

What is there of the divine
in a load of bricks?

What is there of the divine
in a barber's shop?...

Much.

All.

Is not
Solomon's temple built
because
Solomon is not a temple,
but a brothel and a changehouse?

Is not
the meeting-house dedicated
because men are not?

Is not
the church opened and filled
on Sunday
because the commandments
are not
kept by the worshippers
on Monday?

But when he who worships there,
speaks the truth,
follows the truth,
is the truth's;
when he awakes
by actual communion
to the faith
that God is in him,
will he need
any temple,
any prayer?

August 1834, age 31

If the doctrine
that God is in man
were faithfully taught
and received,

if I lived to speak the truth
and enact it,

if I pursued
every generous sentiment
as one enamoured,

if the majesty of goodness
were reverenced,

would not such a principle serve me
by way of police
at least as well
as a Connecticut Sunday?

August 1834, age 31

No art can exceed the mellow beauty
of one square rood of ground
in the woods this afternoon.

The noise of the locust, the bee, and the pine;
the light, the insect forms,
butterflies, cankerworms hanging,
balloon-spiders swinging,
devils-needles cruising,
chirping grasshoppers;

the tints and forms of the leaves and trees—
not a flower
but its form seems a type,
not a capsule
but it is an elegant seed box—

then the myriad asters, polygalas, and golden-rods,
and through the bush
the far pines,
and overhead
the eternal sky.
All the pleasing forms of art
are imitations of these,
and yet
before the beauty of a right action
all this beauty is cold
and unaffecting.

September 1834, age 31

I rejoice in Time.

I do not cross the common
without a wild poetic delight,
notwithstanding the prose of my demeanour.

Thank God I live in the country.

The maker of a sentence,
like the other artist,
launches out
into the infinite
and builds
a road into Chaos
and old Night,
and is followed
by those who hear him
with something of wild,
creative delight.

It is very easy in the world
to live by the opinion
of the world.

It is very easy in solitude
to be self-centered.

But the finished man
is he who in the midst of the crowd
keeps with perfect sweetness
the independence of solitude.

Excite the soul,
and it becomes suddenly virtuous.

Touch the deep heart,
and all these listless, stingy,
beef-eating bystanders
will see the dignity of a sentiment;
will say,
This is good,
and all I have I will give for that.

Excite the soul,
and the weather and the town
and your condition in the world
all disappear;
the world itself loses its solidity,
nothing remains
but the soul
and the Divine Presence
in which it lives.

The Teacher
that I look for and await
shall enunciate with more precision
and universality,
with piercing poetic insight
those beautiful
yet severe compensations
that give to moral nature
an aspect of mathematical science.

He
will not occupy himself
in laboriously reanimating
a historical religion,
but in bringing men to God
by showing them
that he is,
not was,
and speaks,
not spoke.

Who can tell
the moment
when the pine outgrew
the whortleberry
that shaded its first sprout.

It went by
in the night.

Do you see what we preserve of history?
a few anecdotes
of a moral quality
of some momentary act or word—
the word of Canute on the seashore,
the speech of the Druid to Edwin,
the anecdote of Alfred's learning
to read for Judith's gift,
the box on the ear by the herdsman's wife,
the tub of Diogenes,
the gold of Croesus,
and Solon, and Cyrus,
the emerald of Polycrates;
these things, reckoned insignificant
at the age of their occurrence,
have floated,
whilst laws and expeditions and books
and kingdoms
have sunk
and are forgotten.

October 1835, age 32

Charles thinks
if a superior being
should look into families,
he would find natural relations existing,
and man a worthy being,
but if he followed them
into shops, senates, churches, and societies,
they would appear
wholly artificial and worthless.

Society seems noxious.

I believe
that against these baleful influences
Nature is the antidote.
The man comes out of the wrangle
of the shop and office,
and sees the sky and the woods,
and is a man again.

He not only quits the cabal,
but he finds himself.
But how few men see the sky and the woods!

February 1836, age 32

Beautiful morn,
follower
of a beautiful moon.

Yet lies the snow
on the ground.

Birds sing,
mosses creep,
grass grows
on the edge
of the snow-bank.

I gladly pay the rent of my house
because
I therewith get
the horizon
and the woods
which I pay no rent for.

For daybreak and evening and night,
I pay no tax.

I think it is a glorious bargain
which I drive with the town.

.

Today came to me
the first proof-sheet
of *Nature*
to be corrected,
like a new coat,
full of vexations;
with the first sentences
of the chapters perched
like mottoes
aloft
in small type!

The peace of the author
cannot be wounded
by such trifles,
if he sees
that the sentences are still good.

A
good
sentence
can
never
be
put
out
of
countenance
by
any
blunder
of
compositors.

How many attractions for us
have our passing fellows in the streets,
both male and female,
which our ethics forbid us to express,
which yet infuse
so much pleasure into life.

A lovely child,
a handsome youth,
a beautiful girl,
a heroic man,
a maternal woman,
a venerable old man,
charm us, though strangers,
and we cannot say so,
or look at them
but for a moment.

November 1836, age 33

Cold
April;
hard times;
men breaking
who ought not to break;
banks bullied
into the bolstering of desperate speculators;
all the newspapers
a chorus
of owls.

April 1837, age 33

Sad
is this continual
postponement
of life.

I refuse sympathy
and intimacy with people,
as if in view of some
better sympathy and intimacy to come.
But whence
and when?

I
pluck
golden fruit
from rare meetings
with wise men.

I
can well
abide alone
in the intervals,
and
the fruit
of my own tree
shall have
a better flavor.

May 1837, age 33

Among
provocatives,
the next best thing
to good preaching
is bad preaching.

I have even more thoughts during
or enduring it
than at other times.

We have had
two peerless summer days
after all our cold winds and rains.
I have weeded corn and strawberries,
intent on being fat,
and have foreborne study.
The Maryland yellow-throat
pipes to me all day long,
seeming to say
Ecstasy! Ecstasy!
and the Bob-o'-Lincoln
flies and sings.

May 1837, age 34

Overhead
the sanctities of the stars shine forevermore,
and to me also,
pouring satire
on the pompous business of the day
which they close,
and making the generations of men
show slight
and evanescent.

A man is
but a bug,
the earth
but a boat,
a cockle,
drifting
under their old light.

It is not all books
which it behooves him [the scholar] to know,
least of all to be a book-worshipper,
but he must be able to read
in all books
that which alone gives value to books—
in all
to read one,
the one incorruptible text
of truth.

An enchanting night
of south wind and clouds;
mercury at 73°;
all the trees are wind-harps;
blessed be light and darkness;
ebb and flow,
cold and heat;
these restless pulsations
of nature
which
by and by
will throb no more.

After raffling all day
in Plutarch's morals,
or shall I say
angling there,
for such fish as I might find,
I sallied out
this fine afternoon
through the woods
to Walden water.

August 1837, age 34

They say
the insane like a master;
so always does
the human heart
hunger after
a leader,
a master
through truth.

I believe
I shall some time
cease
to be
an individual,
that the eternal tendency
of the soul
is
to become
Universal...

I said when I awoke,
After some more sleepings and wakings
I shall lie on this mattress sick;
then, dead;
and through my gay entry
they will carry these bones.

Where shall I be then?

I lifted my head
and beheld the spotless orange light
of the morning
beaming up
from the dark hills
into the wide Universe.

October 1837, age 34

It is
very hard
to be
simple
enough
to be good.

'Miracles have ceased.'

Have they indeed?
When?

They had not ceased this afternoon
when I walked into the wood
and got into bright,
miraculous sunshine,
in shelter from the roaring wind.

Who sees a pine-cone,
or the turpentine exuding from the tree,
or a leaf, the unit of vegetation,
fall from its bough,
as if it said,
'the year is finished,'
or hears in the quiet, piny glen
the chickadee
chirping his cheerful note,
or walks along the lofty
promontory-like ridges
which, like natural causeways,
traverse the morass,
or gazes upward at the rushing clouds,
or downward at a moss or a stone
and says to himself,
'Miracles have ceased'?

Tell me, good friend,

November 1837, age 34

when this hillock on which your foot stands
swelled from the level of the sphere
by volcanic force;
pick up that pebble at your foot;
look at its gray sides,
its sharp crystal,
and tell me what fiery inundation of the world
melted the minerals like wax,
and, as if the globe were one glowing crucible,
gave this stone its shape.

There is the truth-speaking pebble itself,
to affirm to endless ages
the thing was so.

Tell me where is the manufactory of this air,
so thin, so blue, so restless,
which eddies around you,
in which your life floats,
of which your lungs
are but an organ,
and which you coin into musical words.

I am agitated with curiosity
to know the secret of nature.

Why cannot geology,
why cannot botany
speak and tell me
what has been, what is,
as I run along the forest promontory,

November 1837, age 34

and ask when it rose
like a blister on heated steel?

Then I looked up and saw the sun
shining in the vast sky,
and heard the wind bellow above
and the water glistened in the vale.

These were the forces
that wrought then
and work now.

Yes, there they grandly speak
to all
plainly,
in proportion as we are
quick to apprehend.

November 1837, age 34

I do not like
to see a sword
at a man's side.

If it threaten man,
it threatens me.

A company of soldiers
is an offensive spectacle.

My good Henry Thoreau
made this else solitary afternoon
sunny
with his simplicity
and clear perception.

How comic
is simplicity
in this double-dealing,
quacking world.

Everything that boy says
makes merry with society,
though nothing can be graver
than his meaning.

How much self-reliance
it implies
to write a true description
of anything,
for example,
Wordsworth's picture of skating;
that leaning back on your heels
and stopping
in mid-career.

So simple a fact
no common man
would have trusted himself
to detach
as a thought.

February 1838, age 34

Ah! could I have felt
in the presence of the first,
as now I feel,
my own power and hope,
and so have offered her
in every word and look
the heart of a man humble and wise,
but resolved
to be true and perfect
with God,
and not, as I fear it seemed,
the uneasy, uncentered joy
of one who received in her a good
—a lovely good—
out of all proportion to his deserts,
I might haply have made her days
longer and certainly sweeter,
and at least have recalled
her seraph smile
without a pang.

March 1838, age 34

Yesterday afternoon I went to the Cliff
with Henry Thoreau.
Warm, pleasant, misty weather,
which the great mountain amphitheatre
seemed to drink in with gladness.
A crow's voice
filled all the miles of air with sound.
A bird's voice,
even a piping frog,
enlivens a solitude
and makes world enough for us.

April 1838, age 34

At night I went out into the dark
and saw a glimmering star
and heard a frog,
and Nature seemed to say,
Well, do not these suffice?
Here is a new scene, a new experience.
Ponder it, Emerson,
and not like the foolish world,
hanker after thunders
and multitudes
and vast landscapes,
the sea or Niagara.

April 1838, age 34

A Bird-while.
In a natural chronometer,
a Bird-while
may be admitted as one
of the metres,
since the space most of the wild birds
will allow you to make your observations
on them when they alight near you
in the woods,
is a pretty
equal
and
familiar
measure.

Dark though the hour be,
and dull the wit,
no flood of thoughts,
no lovely pictures
in memory
or in hope,
only heavy, weary duty,
moving on cart-wheels
along the old ruts of life—
I will still trust.

May 1838, age 34

Come out of your warm,
angular house,
resounding with few voices,
into the chill, grand, instantaneous night,
with such a Presence
as a full moon in the clouds,
and you are struck with poetic wonder.
In the instant you leave far behind
all human relations,
wife, mother and child,
and live only with the savages—
water, air, light, carbon, lime, and granite

I become a moist, cold element.

Frogs pipe; waters far off tinkle;
dry leaves hiss; grass bends and rustles,
and I have died
out of the human world
and come to feel
a strange, cold, aqueous, terraqueous, aerial,
ethereal sympathy and existence.
I sow the sun and moon for seeds.

May 1838, age 34

In the wood,
God was manifest,
as he was not in the sermon.
In the cathedralled larches
the ground-pine crept him,
the thrush sung him,
the robin complained him,
the cat-bird mewed him,
the anemone vibrated him,
the wild apple bloomed him;
the ants built their little Timbuctoo wide abroad;
the wild grapes budded;
the rye was in the blade;
high overhead, high over cloud,
the faint, sharp-horned moon sailed steadily west
through fleets of little clouds;
the sheaves of the birch brightened into green below.
The pines kneaded their aromatics in the sun.
All prepared itself
for the warm thunder-days
of July.

May 1838, age 35

A man
must have aunts and cousins,
must buy carrots and turnips,
must have barn and woodshed,
must go to market
and to the blacksmith's shop,
must saunter and sleep
and
be inferior and silly.

Mercury 90° in the shade.

Rivers of heat, yea,
a circumambiant sea.
Welcome as truly
as finer and coarser influences
to this mystic, solitary 'purple island'
that I am!
I celebrate the holy hour at church
amid these fine creative
deluges of light and heat
which evoke so many gentle traits
—gentle and bold—
in man and woman.

Man in summer is Man intensated.

June 1838, age 35

Animal magnetism peeps.
If an adept
should attempt
to put me to sleep
by the concentration of his will
without my leave,
I should feel
unusual rights
over that person's
person
and life.

Keep away from keyholes.

June 1838, age 35

Let a minister wear a cane,
or a white hat,
go to a theatre,
or avoid a Sunday School,
let a school-book with a Calvinistic sentence
or a Sunday School book without one
be heard of,
and instantly all the old grannies
squeak and gibber
and do what they call 'sounding an alarm,'
from Bangor to Mobile.

The moon and Jupiter side by side
last night stemmed the sea of clouds
and plied their voyage in convoy
through the sublime Deep
as I walked the old and dusty road.

The snow and the enchantment of the moonlight
make all landscapes alike,
and the road that is so tedious and homely
that I never take it by day—
by night is Italy or Palmyra.

In these divine pleasures permitted to me
of walks in the June night
under moon and stars,
I can put my life as a fact before me
and stand aloof from its honor and shame.

June 1838, age 35

I went at sundown
to the top of Dr. Ripley's hill
and renewed my vows
to the Genius of that place.

Somewhat of awe,
somewhat grand and solemn
mingles with the beauty
that shines afar around.

In the West,
where the sun was sinking behind clouds,
one pit of splendor lay
as in a desert of space, a deposit
of still light, not radiant.
Then I beheld the river,
like God's love,
journeying out of the grey past
on into the green future.

September 1838, age 35

Sincerity
is the highest compliment
you can pay.

Jones Very
charmed us all
by telling us
he hated us all.

There are some men
above grief
and some men
below it.

What is the hardest task in the world?

To think . . . .

'Tis pity
we should leave with the children
all the romance,
all that is daintiest in life,
and reserve for ourselves
as we grow old
only the prose.

May 1839, age 36

My life is a May game,
I will live as I like.
I defy
your straight-laced,
weary, social ways and modes.
Blue is the sky,
green the fields and groves,
fresh the springs,
glad the rivers,
and hospitable the splendor of sun and star.
I will play my game out.

Love
is
thaumaturgic.
It converts a chair,
a box,
a scrap of paper,
or a line carelessly drawn on it,
a lock of hair,
a faded weed,
into amulets
worth the world's fee.

June 1839, age 36

I know no means of calming
the fret and perturbation
into which
too much sitting,
too much talking,
brings me,
so perfect
as labor.

I have no animal spirits;
therefore,
when surprised by company
and kept in a chair for many hours,
my heart sinks,
my brow is clouded
and I think I will run for Acton woods,
and live with the squirrels
henceforward.

But my garden is nearer,
and my good hoe,
as it bites the ground,
revenges my wrongs,
and I have less lust
to bite my enemies.

I confess I work at first with a little venom,
lay to a little unnecessary strength.

June 1839, age 36

But by smoothing the rough hillocks,
I smooth my temper,
by extracting the long roots of the piper-grass,
I draw out my own splinters;
and in a short time
I can hear the bobolink's song
and see the blessed deluge
of light
and colour
that rolls around me.

June 1839, age 36

It is one of the signs
of our time,
the ill health of all people.

All the young people
are nearsighted
in the towns.

I like my boy,
with his endless, sweet soliloquies
and iterations,
and his utter inability to conceive
why
I should not leave
all my nonsense business and writing,
and come to tie up his toy horse,
as if there was or could be
any end to nature
beyond his horse.

Night
in this enchanting season
is not night,
but a miscellany
of lights.
The journeying twilight,
the half-moon,
the kindling Venus,
the beaming Jove,
Saturn and Mars something less bright,
and, fainter still,
'the common people of the sky,'
...then, below,
the meadows and thickets
flashing with the fireflies,
and all around
the farms the steadier lamps of men
compose the softest, warmest illumination.

July 1839, age 36

When I was thirteen years old,
my Uncle Samuel Ripley
one day asked me,

'How is it, Ralph, that all
the boys dislike you
and quarrel with you,
whilst the grown people are fond of you?'

Now am I thirty-six
and the fact is reversed—
the old people suspect
and dislike me,
and the young love me.

Who can blame men
for seeking excitement?

They are polar,
and would you have them sleep
in a dull eternity
of equilibrium?

Religion, love, ambition, money, war, brandy,
—some fierce antagonism
must break the round of perfect circulation
or no spark, no joy, no event can be.
As good not be.

In the country,
the lover of nature
dreaming through the wood
would never awake to thought
if the scream of an eagle,
the cries of a crow or a curlew
near his head,
did not break the continuity.

The world
can never be learned
by learning
all its details.

Some books
leave us free
and
some books
make us free.

We walked this afternoon
to Edmund Hosmer's and Walden Pond.
The South wind blew
and filled with bland and warm light
the dry sunny woods.
The last year's leaves flew
like birds through the air.
As I sat on the bank of the Drop,
or God's Pond,
and saw the amplitude
of the little water,
what space,
what verge,
the little scudding fleets of ripples
found to scatter and spread
from side to side
and take so much time
to cross the pond,
and saw how the water seemed
made for the wind,
and the wind for the water,
dear playfellows for each other—
I said to my companion,
I declare this world is so beautiful
that I can hardly believe it exists.

April 1840, age 36

Sad spectacle
that a man should live
and be fed
that he may fill a paragraph
every year in the newspapers
for his wonderful age,
as we record
the weight and girth
of the Big Ox,
or Mammoth Girl.

We do not count a man's years
until he has nothing else to count.

I finish this morning
transcribing my old essay on Love,
but I see well its inadequateness.
I, cold
because I am hot—
cold at the surface only
as a sort of guard and compensation
for the fluid tenderness of the core,
have much more experience
than I have written there,
more than I will,
more than I can write.
In silence
we must wrap much of our life,
because it is too fine for speech,
because also
we cannot explain it to others,
and because
somewhat
we cannot yet understand.

The language of the street is always strong.
What can describe
the folly and emptiness
of scolding
like the word *jawing*?
I feel too the force of the double negative,
though clean contrary to our grammar rules.
And I confess to some pleasure
from the stinging rhetoric of a rattling oath
in the mouth of truckmen and teamsters.
How laconic and brisk it is
by the side of a page
of the *North American Review*.
Cut these words and they would bleed;
they are vascular and alive;
they walk and run.
Moreover
they who speak them have this elegancy,
that they do not trip in their speech.
It is a shower of bullets,
whilst Cambridge men and Yale men
correct themselves and begin again
every half sentence.

June 1840, age 37

Now for near five years
I have been indulged
by the gracious Heaven
in my long holiday
in this goodly house of mine,
entertaining and entertained
by so many worthy
and gifted friends,
and all this time
poor Nancy Barron,
the mad-woman,
has been screaming herself hoarse
at the Poor-house
across the brook
and I still hear her
whenever I open my window.

I went into the woods.
I found myself
not wholly present there.
If I looked at a pine-tree or an aster,
that did not seem to be Nature.
Nature was still elsewhere:
this, or this was but outskirt
and far-off reflection
and echo of the triumph
that had passed by
and was now at its glancing splendor and heyday,
perchance in the neighboring fields,
or, if I stood in the field,
then in the adjacent woods.

Always
the present object gave me
this sense of the stillness
that follows a pageant
that has just gone by.

September 1840, age 37

A sleeping child
gives me
the impression
of a traveller
in a very far country.

What a pity
that we cannot curse and swear
in good society!

Cannot the stinging dialect
of the sailors be domesticated?

It is the best rhetoric,
and for a hundred occasions
those forbidden words
are the only good ones.

My page about 'Consistency'
would be better written thus:
'Damn Consistency!'

When I look at the sweeping sleet
amid the pine woods,
my sentences look very
contemptible,
and I think I will never write more:
but the words
prompted by an irresistible charity,
the words
whose path
from the heart to the lips
I cannot follow,
are fairer than the snow.
It is pitiful
to be
an artist...

January 1841, age 37

I guard my moods
as anxiously
as a miser his money;
for
company, business,
my own household chores,
untune and disqualify me
for writing.

I think then
the writer ought not to be married;
ought not to have a family.
I think the Roman Church
with its celibate clergy
and its monastic cells
was right.
If he must marry,
perhaps he should be regarded happiest
who has a shrew for a wife,
a sharp-tongued notable dame
who can and will assume
the total economy of the house;
and, having some sense that her philosopher
is best in his study,
suffers him not to intermeddle
with her thrift.

February 1841, age 37

I am sometimes discontented
with my house
because it lies on a dusty road,
and with its sills and cellar
almost in the water of the meadow.
But when I creep out of it
into the Night
or the Morning
and see what majestic
and what tender beauties
daily wrap me
in their bosom,
how near to me
is every transcendent secret
of Nature's love
and religion,
I see how indifferent it is
where I eat and sleep.

June 1841, age 38

This very street
of hucksters and taverns
the moon
will transform
to a Palmyra,
for she
is the apologist
of all apologists,
and will kiss the elm trees
alone
and hides
every meanness
in a silver-edged
darkness.

The borer
on our peach trees
bores
that she may deposit
an egg:
but the borer
into theories
and institutions
and books
bores
that he
may bore.

June 1841, age 38

Do not
waste yourself
in rejection;
do not
bark against the bad,
but chant
the beauty
of the good.

I remember, when a child,
in the pew on Sundays
amusing myself
with saying over common words
as 'black,' 'white,' 'board,' etc.,
twenty or thirty times,
until the word lost all meaning and fixedness,
and I began to doubt
which was the right name for the thing,
when I saw that neither
had any natural relation,
but all were arbitrary.

August 1841, age 38

The trumpet-like
lowing of a cow—
what does that speak to in me?
Not to my understanding.
No.

Yet somewhat in me
hears
and loves it well.

I suppose
there is no more
abandoned epicure
or opium-eater
than I.

I taste every hour
of these autumn days.
Every light from the sky,
every shadow on the earth,
ministers to my pleasure.
I love this gas.
I grudge to move
or to labor
or to change my book
or to will,
lest I should disturb
the sweet dream.

August 1841, age 38

I would have my book read
as I have read my favorite books,
not with explosion and astonishment,
a marvel and a rocket,
but a friendly
and agreeable influence
stealing like the scent of a flower,
or the sight of a new landscape
on a traveller.
I neither wish to be hated and defied
by such as I startle,
nor to be kissed and hugged
by the young
whose thoughts I stimulate.

October 1841, age 38

The sum of life
ought to be valuable
when the fractions and particles
are so sweet.

We are
very near
to greatness:

one step
and we are safe:

can we
not
take the leap?

There is truly but one miracle,
the perpetual fact
of Being and Becoming,
the ceaseless saliency,
the transit from the Vast
to the particular,
which miracle,
one and the same,
has for its most universal name
the word *God*.

Take one or two or three steps
where you will,
from any fact in Nature or Art,
and you come out
full on this fact;
as you may
penetrate the forest
in any direction
and go straight on,
you will
come to the sea.

November 1841, age 38

There came into the house
a young maiden,
but she seemed to be more
than a thousand years old.
She came into the house
naked and helpless,
but she had for her defense
more than the strength of millions.
She brought into the day
the manners of the Night.

All writing
is by the grace of God.
People do not deserve
to have good writing,
they are so pleased with bad.
In these sentences that you show me,
I can find no beauty,
for I see death
in every clause and every word.
There is a fossil or a mummy character
which pervades this book.
The best sepulchres,
the vastest catacombs,
Thebes and Cairo,
Pyramids,
are sepulchres to me.
I like gardens and nurseries.
Give me initiative,
spermatic,
prophesying,
man-making words.

December 1841, age 38

Are you not scared
by seeing
that the Gypsies
are more attractive
to us
than the Apostles?

For though
we love goodness
and not stealing,
yet also we love
freedom
and not preaching.

A saint,
an angel,
a chorus of saints,
a myriad of Christs,
are alike worthless and
forgotten by the soul,
as the leaves that fall,
or the fruit that was
gathered in the garden of Eden
in the golden age.

A new day,
a new harvest,
new duties,
new men,
new fields of thought,
new powers call you,
and an eye fastened on the past
unsuns nature,
bereaves me of hope,
and ruins me
with a squalid indigence
which nothing but death
can adequately symbolize.

April 1842, age 38

If I should write an honest diary,
what should I say?
Alas, that life
has halfness, shallowness.
I have almost completed thirty-nine years,
and I have not yet adjusted
my relation to my fellows on the planet,
or to my own work.
Always too young or too old,
I do not justify myself;
how can I satisfy others?

April 1842, age 38

The man must be
equal to the book.
A man does not know
how fine a morning he wants
until he goes to read
Plato and Proclus.

Some play
at chess,
some
at cards,
some
at the Stock Exchange.
I prefer
to play
at Cause and Effect.

The only poetic fact
in the life of thousands and thousands
is their death.

No wonder
they specify all the circumstances
of the death
of another person.

August 1842, age 39

Last night
a walk to the river
with Margaret,
and saw
the moon
broken
in the water,
interrogating,
interrogating.

The sannup and the squaw
do not get drunk
at the same time.
They take turns
in keeping sober,
and
husband and wife
should never be low-spirited
at the same time,
but each should be able
to cheer the other.

You
shall
have
joy,
or
you
shall
have
power,
said God;
you shall not have both.

Henry Thoreau
made,
last night,
the fine remark
that, as long as a man
stands
in his own way,
everything seems to be in his way,
governments,
society,
and even the sun
and moon
and stars,
as astrology may testify.

Time is the little grey man
who takes out of his breast-pocket
first a pocketbook, then a Dollond telescope,
then a Turkey carpet,
then four saddled and bridled nags
and a sumptuous canvas tent.
We are accustomed to chemistry
and it does not surprise us.
But chemistry is but a name for changes
and developments as wonderful
as those of this Breast-pocket.
I was a little chubby boy
trundling a hoop in Chauncy Place,
and spouting poetry from Scott and Campbell
at the Latin School.
But Time, the little grey man,
has taken out of his vest-pocket
a great, awkward house
(in a corner of which I sit down and write of him)
some acres of land, several full-grown
and several very young persons,
and seated them close beside me;
then he has taken that chubbiness
and that hoop quite away
(to be sure he has left the declamation and the poetry),
and here left a long, lean person
threatening to be a little grey man,
like himself.

November 1842, age 39

Conservatism stands on this,
that a man
cannot jump
out of his skin;
and well for him that he cannot,
for his skin
is the world;
and the stars of heaven
do hold him there:
in the folly of men
glitters
the wisdom of God.

The railroad,
which was
but a toy coach the other day,
is now a dowdy,
lumbering
country wagon...
The Americans
take to the little contrivance
as if it were
the cradle
in which they were born.

Earth Spirit,
living,
a black river
like that swarthy stream
which rushes through the human body
is thy nature,
demoniacal,
warm,
fruitful,
sad,
nocturnal.

Mr. Adams
chose wisely
and
according to his constitution,
when,
on leaving the Presidency,
he
went into Congress.
He is no
literary old gentleman,
but a bruiser,
and loves the mêlée.
When they talk about his age
and venerableness
and nearness to the grave,
he knows better,
he is like one of those old cardinals,
who, as quick as he is chosen Pope,
throws away his crutches
and his crookedness,
and is as straight as a boy.

February 1843, age 39

The philosophers at Fruitlands
have such an image
of virtue
before their eyes,
that the poetry of man and nature
they never see;
the poetry that is in man's life,
the poorest pastoral clownish life;
the light that shines on a man's hat,
in a child's spoon,
the sparkle on every wave
and on every mote of dust,
they see not.

March 1843, age 39

My garden is an honest place.
Every tree and every vine
are incapable
of concealment,
and tell
after two or three months
exactly
what sort of treatment
they have had.
The sower may mistake
and sow his peas crookedly:
the peas make no mistake,
but come up
and show his line.

All the physicians
I have ever seen
call themselves believers,
but are materialists;
they believe only
in the existence of matter,
and not in matter as an appearance,
but as substance,
and do not contemplate a cause.
Their idea of spirit
is a chemical agent.

It is greatest
to believe
and to hope
well
of the world,
because he who does so,
quits the world
of experience,
and makes
the world he lives in.

The sky is the daily bread of the eyes.

Fools and clowns and sots
make the fringes
of every one's tapestry of life,
and give a certain reality to the picture.
What could we do in Concord
without Bigelow's
and Wesson's bar-rooms
and their dependencies?
What without such fixtures as Uncle Sol,
and old Moore
who sleeps in Doctor Hurd's barn,
and the red charity-house
over the brook?
Tragedy and comedy
always go hand in hand.

The sun and the evening sky
do not look calmer
than Alcott and his family
at Fruitlands...
I will not
prejudge them
successful.
They look well in July.
We will see them in December.

Henry Thoreau sends me a paper
with the old fault
of unlimited contradiction.
The trick of his rhetoric
is soon learned:
it consists in substituting
for the obvious word and thought
its diametrical antagonist.
He praises wild mountains and winter forests
for their domestic air;
snow and ice
for their warmth;
villagers and wood-choppers
for their urbanity;
and the wilderness
for resembling Rome and Paris.

August 1843, age 40

The only straight line
in Nature
that I remember
is the spider
swinging down from a twig.

Alcott came,
the magnificent dreamer,
brooding, as ever,
on the renewal
or reëdification
of the social fabric
after ideal law,
heedless
that he had been uniformly rejected
by every class to whom
he has addressed himself,
and just as sanguine and vast as ever...
Very pathetic it is
to see this wandering Emperor
from year to year
making his round of visits
from house to house
of such as do not exclude him,
seeking a companion,
tired of pupils.

We rail at trade,
but the historian of the world
will see
that it was the principle of liberty;
that it settled America,
and
destroyed feudalism,
and
made peace
and
keeps peace;
that it will abolish slavery.

When I address a large assembly,
as last Wednesday,
I am always apprised
what an opportunity is there:
not for reading to them,
as I do,
lively miscellanies,
but for painting in fire
my thought,
and being agitated
to agitate.

February 1844, age 40

If I try
to get many hours
in a day,
I shall not have
any.

I wish to have
rural strength
and religion
for my children,
and I wish city facility
and polish.
I find
with chagrin
that I cannot have both.

Be an opener of doors
for such as come after thee,
and do not try to make the universe
a blind alley.

Alas!
our Penetration increases
as we grow older,
and we are
no longer deceived
by great words
when unrealized
and unembodied.
Say rather,
we detect littleness
in expressions
and thoughts
that once we should have taken
and cited
as proofs of strength.

March 1845, age 41

Good manners
require
a great deal
of time,
as does
a wise treatment
of children.

A few foolish and cunning managers
ride the conscience
of this great country
with their Texas,
or Tariff,
or Democracy,
or other mumbo-jumbo,
and all give in
and are verily persuaded
that that is great—
all else is trifling.
And why?
Because there is really no great life,
and one demonstration
in all the broad land
of that which is
the heart and the soul
of every rational American man—
the mountains walking,
the light incarnated,
reason and virtue clothed in flesh—
he does not see.

March 1845, age 41

Poetry
must be
as new
as foam,
and as old
as the rock.

What argument,
what eloquence
can avail against the power
of that one word
niggers?
The man of the world
annihilates
the whole combined force
of all
the anti-slavery societies of the world
by
pronouncing it.

Life is a game
between God and man.
The one disparts himself
and feigns to divide into individuals.
He puts part in a pomegranate,
part in a king's crown,
part in a person.
Instantly man sees the beautiful things
and goes to procure them.
As he takes down each one
the Lord smiles and says,
It is yourself;
and when he has them all,
it will be *yourself*.

Far the best part,
I repeat,
of every mind
is not that which he knows,
but that which hovers in gleams,
suggestions,
tantalizing, unpossessed,
before him.
His firm recorded knowledge
soon loses all interest for him.
But this dancing chorus
of thoughts
and hopes
is the quarry of his future,
is his possibility,
and teaches him
that his man's life is of a ridiculous brevity
and meanness,
but that it is his first age and trial
only of his young wings,
but that vast revolutions, migrations,
and gyres on gyres
in the celestial societies
invite him.

November 1845, age 42

God
builds
his temple
in the heart
on the ruins
of churches
and religions.

What a discovery I made one day,
that the more I spent
the more I grew,
that it was as easy
to occupy a large place
and do much work
as an obscure place
to do little;
and that in the winter
in which I communicated
all my results to classes,
I was full of new thoughts.

March 1846, age 42

I like man,
but not men.

When summer opens,
I see how fast it matures,
and fear it will be short;
but after the heats of July and August,
I am reconciled,
like one who has had his swing,
to the cool of autumn.
So will it be
with the coming of death.

May 1846, age 42

These rabble at Washington
are really better
than the sniveling opposition.
They have a sort of genius
of a bold and manly cast,
though Satanic.
They see, against the unanimous
expression of the people,
how much a little well-directed
effrontery can achieve,
how much crime the people will bear,
and they proceed
from step to step...

June 1846, age 43

What is the oldest thing?

A dimple
or
whirlpool
in water.
That
is
Genesis,
Exodus,
and all.

'Your reading is irrelevant.'

Yes, for you, but not for me.
It makes no difference what I read.
If it is irrelevant, I read it deeper.
I read it until it is pertinent
to me and mine,
to Nature,
and to the hour that now passes.

A good scholar will find
Aristophanes and Hafiz and Rabelais
full of American history.

I believe in
Omnipresence
and find footsteps
in grammar rules,
in oyster shops,
in church liturgies,
in mathematics,
and in solitudes
and in galaxies.

Work and learn in evil days,
in insulted days,
in days of debt and depression
and calamity.
Fight best
in the shade of the cloud
of arrows.

The days come and go
like muffled
and veiled figures
sent from a distant friendly party,
but they say nothing,
and if we do not use
the gifts they bring,
they carry them
as silently away.

Alas for America,
as I must so often say,
the ungirt,
the diffuse,
the profuse,
procumbent—
one wide ground juniper,
out of which no cedar,
no oak will rear up a mast to the clouds!
It all runs to leaves,
to suckers,
to tendrils,
to miscellany.
The air is loaded with poppy,
with imbecility,
with dispersion and sloth.

Eager,
solicitous,
hungry,
rabid,
busy-bodied
America
attempting many things,
vain,
ambitious
to feel thy own existence,
and convince others of thy talent,
by attempting and hastily accomplishing much;
yes, catch thy breath
and correct thyself,
and failing here,
prosper out there;
speed and fever are never greatness;
but reliance and serenity
and waiting.

June 1847, age 44

The Superstitions of Our Age:

The fear of Catholicism;

The fear of pauperism;

The fear of immigration;

The fear of manufacturing interests;

The fear of radicalism or democracy;

And faith

in the steam engine.

August 1847, age 44

Life consists
in what a man
is
thinking of
all day.

If I should believe
the Reviews,
and I am always
of their opinion,
I have never written anything good.
And yet,
against all criticism,
the books survive
until this day.

Happy is he
who looks
only into his work
to know if it will succeed,
never
into the times
or the public opinion;
and who writes
from the love
of imparting certain thoughts
and not from the necessity of sale—
who writes
always
to *the unknown friend.*

Henry Thoreau
is like the wood-god
who solicits the wandering poet
and draws him into antres vast
and deserts idle,
and bereaves him of his memory,
and leaves him naked,
plaiting vines
and with twigs in his hand...

August 1848, age 45

As for taking
Thoreau's arm,
I should as soon
take the arm
of an elm tree.

August 1848, age 45

I go twice a week over Concord
with Ellery, and, as we sit
on the steep park at Conantum,
we still have the same regret
as oft before.

Is all this beauty to perish?

Shall none remake this sun and wind,
the sky-blue river,
the river-blue sky;
the yellow meadow spotted with sacks
and sheets of cranberry-pickers;
the red bushes;
the iron-gray house
with just the color of the granite rock;
the paths of the thicket,
in which the only engineers
are the cattle
grazing on yonder hill;
the wide, straggling wild orchard
in which Nature has deposited
every possible flavor
in the apples
of different trees?

September 1848, age 45

The salvation of America
and of the human race
depends
on the next election,
if we believe
the newspapers.

But so it was
last year,
and so it was
the year before,
and our fathers believed
the same thing
forty years ago.

October 1848, age 45

Every poem
must be
made up of lines
that are
poems.

Love is necessary
to the righting of the estate
of woman in this world.
Otherwise nature itself
seems to be in conspiracy
against her dignity
and welfare;
for the cultivated, high-thoughted,
beauty-loving, saintly woman
finds herself unconsciously desired for her sex,
and even enhancing the appetite
of her savage pursuers
by these fine ornaments
she has piously laid on herself.
She finds with indignation
that she is herself a snare,
and was made such.
I do not wonder at her occasional protest,
violent protest against nature,
in fleeing to nunneries,
and taking black veils.
Love rights all this deep wrong.

October 1848, age 45

I find out
in an instant
if my companion does not want me;
I cannot comprehend
how my visitor
does not perceive
that I do not want him.
It is his business
to find out that
I, of course,
must be civil.
It is for him to offer to go.

I hate
quotations.
Tell me what you know.

Come hither, youth,
and learn
how the brook that flows
at the bottom of your garden,
or the farmer
who ploughs the adjacent field,
your father and mother,
your debts and credits,
and your web of habits
are the very best basis of poetry,
and the material
which you must work up.

Like the New England soil,
my talent is good
only
whilst I work it.
If I cease to task myself,
I have no thoughts.

This is a poor sterile Yankeeism.
What I admire and love
is
the generous and spontaneous soil
which flowers and fruits
at all seasons.

December 1849, age 46

It is a vulgar error to suppose
that a gentleman must be ready
to fight.
The utmost that can be demanded of the gentleman
is that he be incapable of a lie.
There is a man who has good sense,
is well informed, well read,
obliging, cultivated, capable,
and has an absolute devotion to truth.
He always means what he says,
and says what he means,
however courteously.
You may spit upon him;
nothing could induce him to spit upon you,
no praises, and no possessions,
no compulsion of public opinion.
You may kick him—
he will think it the kick of a brute:
but he is not a brute,
and will not kick you in return.
But neither your knife and pistol,
nor your gifts and courting
will ever make
the smallest impression on his vote or word;
for he is the truth's man,
and will speak and act the truth
until he dies.

December 1849, age 46

Love is temporary
and ends
with marriage.
Marriage is the perfection
which
love aimed at,
ignorant of what it sought.

Marriage is a good
known only to the parties—
a relation of perfect understanding,
aid, contentment,
possession
of themselves
and of the world—
which dwarfs love to green fruit.

The fate of my books
is like
the impression of my face.
My acquaintances,
as long back as I can remember,
have always said,
"Seems to me
you look
a little thinner
than when I saw you last."

The world wears well.
These autumn afternoons
and
well-marbled landscapes
of green and gold and russet,
and steel-blue river,
and smoke-blue New Hampshire mountains,
are
and remain
as bright and perfect penciling
as ever.

Thoreau
wants a little ambition
in his mixture.
Fault of this,
instead of being
the head
of American engineers,
he is captain
of
huckleberry party.

It would be hard to recall
the rambles of last night's talk
with Henry Thoreau.
But we stated over again,
to sadness almost,
the eternal loneliness...
But how insular
and pathetically solitary
are all the people we know!

October 1851, age 48

I think that a man
should
compare advantageously
with a river,
with an oak,
with a mountain,
endless flow,
expansion,
and grit.

Little things are often filled
with great beauty.
The cigar
makes visible the respiration of the body,
an universal fact,
of which the ebb and flow of the sea-tide
is only one example.

To what base uses
we put
this ineffable intellect!
To reading
all day
murders
and railroad accidents,
to choosing
patterns
for waistcoats and scarfs.

May 1852, age 48

The head of Washington
hangs in my dining-room
for a few days past,
and I cannot keep my eyes off of it.
It has a certain Appalachian strength,
as if it were truly
the first-fruits of America,
and expressed the Country.
The heavy, leaden eyes turn on you,
as the eyes of an ox in a pasture.
And the mouth has gravity
and depth of quiet,
as if this MAN had absorbed
all the serenity of America,
and left none
for his restless, rickety, hysterical
countrymen.

July 1852, age 49

I am my own man
more than most men,
yet the loss of a few persons
would be impoverishing—
a few persons
who give flesh
to what were, else,
mere thoughts,
and which now I am not at liberty to slight,
or in any manner
treat as fictions.
It were too much to say
that the Platonic world
I might have learned to treat as cloud-land
had I not known Alcott,
who is a native of that country,
yet I will say that he makes it
as solid as Massachusetts to me ;
and Thoreau gives me,
in flesh and blood
and pertinacious Saxon belief,
my own ethics.
He is far more real,
and daily practically
obeying them,
than I.

July 1852, age 49

The shoemakers and fisherman say
in their shops,
'Damn learning! it spoils the boy;
as soon as he gets a little,
he won't work.'
'Yes,' answers Lemuel, 'but there is learning
somewhere, and somebody
will have it,
and who has it
will have the power,
and will rule you:
knowledge is power.
Why not, then, let your son get it,
as well as another?'

October 1852, age 49

If I have a message to send,
I prefer the telegraph to the wheelbarrow.

I admire answers
to which
no answer can be made.

Rest on your humanity,
and it will supply you
with strength
and hope and vision for the day.
Solitude and the country,
books, and openness,
will feed you;
but go into the city—
I am afraid there is no morning in Chestnut Street,
it is full of rememberers,
they shun each other's eyes,
they are all wrinkled with memory
of the tricks they have played,
or mean to play,
each other,
of petty arts and aims
all contracting and lowering
their aspect and character.

September 1853, age 50

We shall pass
for what we are.
Do not fear to die
because
you have not done your task.
Whenever a noble soul comes,
the audience awaits.
And he is not judged by his performance,
but
by the spirit of his performance....

March 1854, age 50

The lesson of these days
is the vulgarity of wealth.
We know that wealth
will vote for the same thing
which the worst and meanest of the people vote for.
Wealth will vote for rum,
will vote for tyranny,
will vote for slavery,
will vote against the ballot,
will vote against international copyright,
will vote against schools, colleges,
or any high direction of public money.

March 1854, age 50

Shall we
judge the country
by the majority
or by the minority?
Certainly,
by the minority.
The mass are animal,
in state of pupilage,
and nearer
the chimpanzee.

**All
the thoughts
of a turtle
are turtle.**

Jones Very,
who thought it an honour
to wash his own face,
seems to me
less insane
than men who hold
themselves cheap.

Don't let them eat their seed-corn;
don't let them anticipate, ante-date,
and be young men,
before they have finished their boyhood.
Let them have the fields and woods,
and learn their secret
and the base-and foot-ball,
and wrestling, and brickbats,
and suck all the strength and courage
that lies for them in these games;
let them ride bare-back,
and catch their horse in his pasture,
let them hook and spear their fish,
and shin a post and a tall tree,
and shoot their partridge
and trap the woodchuck,
before they begin to dress like collegians
and sing in serenades,
and make polite calls.

May 1856, age 52

Yesterday to the Sawmill Brook
with Henry.
He was in search
of yellow violet (*pubescens*) and *menyanthes*
which he waded into the water for;
and which he concluded
on examination,
had been out five days.
Having found his flowers,
he drew
out of his breast pocket
his diary
and read the names of all the plants
that should bloom this day,
May 20;
whereof he keeps account
as a banker when his notes fall due;
Rubus triflora, Quercus, Vaccinium, etc.
The *Cypripedium*
not due till tomorrow.
...He thinks he could tell
by the flowers
what day of the month it is,
within two days.

May 1856, age 52

And behold the sea,
the opaline,
plentiful and strong,
yet beautiful as the rose or the rainbow,
full of food, nourisher of men,
purger of the world,
creating a sweet climate,
and, in its unchangeable ebb and flow,
and in its beauty at a few furlongs,
giving a hint of that which changes not,
and is perfect.

Because our education is defective,
because we are superficial and ill-read,
we are forced to make the most
of that position, of ignorance.

Hence America
is a vast know-nothing party,
and we disparage books,
and cry up intuition.

With a few clever men
we have made a reputable thing of that,
and denouncing libraries
and severe culture,
and magnifying the mother-wit swagger
of bright boys from the country colleges,
we have even come so far
as to deceive everybody,
except ourselves,
into an admiration
of un-learning and inspiration,
forsooth.

Yesterday,
the best day of the year,
we spent in the afternoon on the river.
A sky of Calcutta;
light,
air,
clouds,
water,
banks,
birds,
grass,
pads,
lilies,
were in perfection,
and it was delicious to live.

I can count
on my fingers
all
the sane men
that ever came to me.

It is impossible to be a gentleman,
and not be an abolitionist.

I see few intellectual persons,
and even those
to no purpose,
and sometimes believe
that I have no new thoughts,
and that my life
is quite at an end.
But the magnet that lies in my drawer,
for years,
may believe it has no magnetism,
and, on touching it with steel,
it knows the old virtue;
and, this morning,
came by a man
with knowledge
and interests like mine,
in his head,
and suddenly
I had thoughts again.

I have been writing and speaking
what were once called novelties,
for twenty-five or thirty years,
and have not now one disciple.

Why?

Not that what I said was not true;
not that it has not found intelligent receivers;
but because it did not go from any wish in me
to bring men to me,
but to themselves.
I delight in driving them from me.
What could I do, if they came to me?
—they would interrupt and encumber me.

This is my boast
that I have no school follower.
I should account it a measure
of the impurity of insight,
if it did not create independence.

The
believing
we do something
when
we do nothing
is
the first
illusion of
tobacco.

I reached the other day
the end of my fifty-seventh year,
and am easier in my mind
than hitherto.
I could never give much reality
to evil and pain.
But now
when my wife says
perhaps this tumor on your shoulder is a cancer,
I say,
What if it is?

Do thy duty of the day.
Just now,
the supreme public duty
of all thinking men
is to assert freedom.
Go where it is threatened,
and say,
'I am for it,
and do not wish to
live in the world
a moment longer
than it exists.'

I read many friendly
and many hostile paragraphs
in the journals
about my new book,
but seldom or never
a just criticism...
I often think
I could write
a criticism on Emerson
that would hit the white.

One capital advantage of old age
is the absolute insignificance
of a success more or less.

The war goes on
educating us
to a trust
in the simplicities,
and to see
the bankruptcy
of all narrow views.

August 1861, age 58

War,
the searcher of character,
the test of men,
has tried already
so many reputations,
has pricked
so many bladders.
'Tis like the financial crises,
which, once in ten or twenty years,
come to try the men and institutions of trade;
using, like them,
no ceremony,
but plain laws
of gravity and force
to try tension and resistance.

March 1862, age 58

I like people
who can do things.
When Edward and I struggled
in vain
to drag our big calf
into the barn,
the Irish girl
put her finger
into the calf's mouth,
and
led her in
directly.

Henry Thoreau remains erect,
calm, self-subsistent,
before me,
and I read him
not only truly in his Journal,
but he is not
long out of mind
when I walk,
and,
as to-day,
row upon the pond.

How shallow seemed to me
yesterday in the woods
the speech one often hears
from tired citizens
who have spent their brief enthusiasm
for the country,
that Nature is tedious,
and they have had enough of green leaves.
Nature and the green leaves
are a million fathoms deep,
and it is these eyes
that are superficial.

August 1862, age 59

I grieve
to see
that the Government
is governed
by the hurrahs
of the soldiers
or the citizens.
It does not lead opinion,
but follows it.

When I bought my farm,
I did not know
what a bargain I had
in the bluebirds, bobolinks, and thrushes;
as little did I know
what sublime mornings
and sunsets
I was buying.

How partial,
like mutilated eunuchs,
the musical artists
appear to me in society!
Politics,
bankruptcy,
frost,
famine,
war—
nothing concerns them but a scraping on a catgut,
or tooting
on a bass French horn.

The human mind
cannot be burned
nor bayonetted,
nor wounded,
nor missing.

In reading Henry Thoreau's journal,
I am very sensible of the vigour of his constitution.
That oaken strength
which I noted whenever he walked,
or worked, or surveyed wood-lots,
the same unhesitating hand
with which a field-labourer accosts a piece of work,
which I should shun as a waste of strength,
Henry shows in his literary task.
He has muscle,
and ventures on and performs feats
which I am forced to decline.
In reading him,
I find the same thought,
the same spirit that is in me,
but he takes a step beyond,
and illustrates
by excellent images
that which I should have conveyed
in a sleepy generality.
'Tis as if I went into a gymnasium,
and saw youths leap, climb, and swing
with a force unapproachable—
though their feats
are only continuations
of my initial grapplings and jumps.

June 1863, age 60

Within,
I do not find
wrinkles
and used heart,
but
unspent
youth.

Old age brings
along with its uglinesses
the comfort that you will soon be out of it—
which ought to be a substantial relief
to such discontented pendulums as we are.
To be out of the war,
out of debt,
out of the drouth, out of the blues,
out of the dentist's hands,
out of the second thoughts,
mortifications, and remorses
that inflict such twinges
and shooting pains,
out of the next winter,
and the high prices,
and company below your ambition,
surely these are soothing hints.
And, harbinger of this,
what an alleviator
is sleep,
which muzzles
all these dogs for me
every day?

July 1864, age 61

There is an astonishing magnificence
even in this low town,
and within a quarter of a mile of my doors,
in the appearance of the Lincoln hills
now drest in their colored forest,
under the lights and clouds of morning,
as I saw them at eight o'clock.
When I see this spectacle so near,
and so surprising,
I think
no house should be built quite low,
or should obstruct the prospect
by trees.

October 1864, age 61

America
should affirm
and establish
that in no instance
should the guns
go
in advance
of the perfect right.

I can find my biography in every fable that I read.

I confess there is sometimes a caprice in fame,
like the unnecessary eternity
given to these minute shells
and antediluvian fishes,
leaves, ferns, yea, ripples and raindrops,
which have come safe down through a vast antiquity,
with all its shocks, upheavals, deluges, and volcanoes,
wherein everything noble
in art and humanity
had perished,
yet these snails, periwinkles, and worthless dead leaves
come staring and perfect into our daylight.
What is Fame,
if every snail
or ripple
or raindrop
shares it?

Success in your work,
the finding a better method,
the better understanding
that insures the better performing
is hat and coat,
is food and wine,
is fire and horse and health and holiday.

You complain
that the Negroes are a base class.

Who makes and keeps
the Jew
or the Negro
base,
who but you,
who exclude them from the rights
which others enjoy?

The only place
where I feel
the joy of eminent domain
is in my woodlot.
My spirits rise whenever I enter it.
I can spend the entire day there
with hatchet or pruning-shears
making paths,
without a remorse of wasting time.
I fancy the birds know me,
and even the trees make little speeches
or hint them.

Autumn 1868, age 65

Culture is one thing,
and varnish another.
There can be no high culture
without pure morals.
With the truly cultivated man—
the maiden,
the orphan,
the poor man,
and the hunted slave
feel safe.

God had infinite time
to give us;
but how did He give it?

In one immense tract
of a lazy millennium?

No, but He cut it up
into neat succession
of new mornings,
and, with each, therefore,
a new idea,
new inventions,
and new applications.

My new book sells faster, it appears,
than either of its foregoers.
This is not for its merit,
but only shows
that old age is a good advertisement.

Your name has been seen so often
that your book must be worth buying.

Look sharply
after your thoughts.
They come unlooked for,
like a new bird
seen on your trees,
and, if you turn to your usual task,
disappear;
and you shall never find
that perception again;
never, I say,
but perhaps years,
ages,
and I know not
what events
and worlds may lie
between you
and its return!

House burned.

The secret
of poetry
is never explained,
is always new.
We have not got farther
than mere wonder
at the delicacy of the touch,
and the eternity it inherits.

I dedicate my book to the Spirit of America.

July 1822, age 19

How This Book Came About

One book leads to another, sometimes ten others. This one came about one spring afternoon when John Dugdale, the famed, "blind" photographer, came to see me with a pile of his blue-toned cyanotypes. Hyperion Press wanted to publish his pictures but John wanted them to be accompanied by text from the Transcendentalists. Would I do it?

Since I was deeply enmeshed in developing a school, putting on a play, starting a new business and completing three books and planning seven others, I said yes!

Like a dragnet I went through the work of Emerson, Thoreau, and Alcott, as well as Walt Whitman and Emily Dickinson. Since it was a favor, no money mentioned, I did not stint. At the end of two weeks I knew the only author on the same beam as John was the irrepressible Henry David Thoreau. His words swelled the power of the pictures and the pictures deepened the power of the words.

Rather than use the old quotes out of Walden I culled selections from Henry David's journals—out of a copy of his journal jottings I'd found in a New Hampshire thrift shop for a dime. I soon had a book—with a beautiful sequence of photos, apt words from the journals, an intro and bios of Thoreau and Dugdale—entitled *New Suns Will Arise.*

New Suns impressed people. The American Library Association nominated it as one of the *Best Books for Young Adults in 2002.* But in reading the published version, I only saw what could have been done with the book.

What disappointed me most was the way they caged in Thoreau. His words were locked in cell-blocks of text when they cried out for space, for breathing room. They wanted to soar. But one must leave the past to the past. I looked to the future, and as an experiment I arranged Thoreau's words as if he were speaking them, in an easy free verse. When I showed them to some people they gasped. The arrangement of the words allowed the impact and profundity of the passages to get free. That experiment became the basis for the upcoming volume—*Thoroughly Thoreau.*

This was the way to get Thoreau out there—out among ordinary people. After all, most of us aren't going to go to libraries and scour through musty volumes of his journals. His thoughts could fly from his head to ours, from his heart to our hearts.

Why not do the same for Emerson? I approached his intimate journals with an open heart and was ignited. With the bicentennial of his birth around the corner, people might open up to the great sage of Concord, the burning light of American spirituality. The result is this book—*Emphatically Emerson.*

Listen to the man breathe out his thoughts.

—Frank Crocitto

Also available by Frank Crocitto from

CANDLEPOWER

NEW SUNS WILL ARISE
FROM THE JOURNALS OF
HENRY DAVID THOREAU
ISBN 0-7868053-9-0

"Crocitto's selections make Thoreau's passion
for living life to the fullest accessible to
a new generation of young readers."
—*Western Washington University*

Recommended by **YALSA** as one of
the **Best Books For Young Adults of 2001**

PUBLISHED BY HYPERION

AVAILABLE FROM CANDLEPOWER

WWW.CANDLEPOWER.ORG

P.O. BOX 787
NEW PALTZ, NY 12561
888-744-1317

INFO@CANDLEPOWER.ORG